Palm Tree

By Simon Ipoo
Illustrated by Rob Owen

Library For All Ltd.

LIBRARY FOR ALL
DIGITAL EDUCATION · FOR THE WORLD

Library For All is an Australian not for profit organisation with a mission to make knowledge accessible to all via an innovative digital library solution. Visit us at libraryforall.org

Palm Tree

This edition published 2022

Published by Library For All Ltd
Email: info@libraryforall.org
URL: libraryforall.org

Library For All gratefully acknowledges the contributions of all who made previous editions of this book possible.

African Storybook.org

www.africanstorybook.org

Original illustrations by Rob Owen

Palm Tree
Ipoo, Simon
ISBN: 978-1-922918-02-4
SKU03030

Palm Tree

2

Let me tell you about the palm tree.

This tree lives when everything else is dry.

The shade from a palm tree is always cool.

We eat fruit from the palm tree.

We use palm leaves to thatch our houses.

We make brooms and mats from palm leaves.

We use palm tree seeds for fuel.

Do you see why the
palm tree is important?

You can use these questions to talk about this book with your family, friends and teachers.

What did you learn from this book?

Describe this book in one word. Funny? Scary? Colourful? Interesting?

How did this book make you feel when you finished reading it?

What was your favourite part of this book?

download our reader app
getlibraryforall.org

About the contributors

Library For All works with authors and illustrators from around the world to develop diverse, relevant, high quality stories for young readers. Visit libraryforall.org for the latest news on writers' workshop events, submission guidelines and other creative opportunities.

Did you enjoy this book?

We have hundreds more expertly curated original stories to choose from.

We work in partnership with authors, educators, cultural advisors, governments and NGOs to bring the joy of reading to children everywhere.

Did you know?

We create global impact in these fields by embracing the United Nations Sustainable Development Goals.

librarand.org

www.ingramcontent.com/pod-product-compliance
Lightning Source LLC
Chambersburg PA
CBHW040320050426
42452CB00018B/2943